YVONN[E]

ALL BY MYSELF

Illustrated by Clare Harrison

DRAGON
GRAFTON BOOKS
A Division of the Collins Publishing Group

LONDON GLASGOW
TORONTO SYDNEY AUCKLAND

Dragon
Grafton Books
A Division of the Collins Publishing Group
8 Grafton Street, London W1X 3LA

Published by Dragon Books 1986

British Library Cataloguing in Publication Data
Whitaker, Yvonne
All by myself.
1. Cookery—Juvenile literature
I. Title
641.5   TX652.5

ISBN 0–583–30911–9

Printed and bound in Great Britain by
Collins, Glasgow

Set in Palatino

For my children
Victoria, Thomas, and Edward

my husband
James

my family

and all our friends

CONTENTS

*numbers after the names of dishes refer to
the age of capability guidance*

ABOUT THIS BOOK

For Parents

Every child from approximately three years upwards wants to help in the kitchen. Parents are keen that their children should experiment with cooking but are worried about the safety aspect. Dealing with hot ovens and hobs can be dangerous, and therefore normal cooking from recipe books needs parental supervision which can be very time consuming. This is a totally different style of cookery book for children aged 4 and upwards. The book contains 82 recipes and none of them require the use of cooker or hob. The child can therefore 'cook' without supervision in complete safety.

Although no direct heat is used, some recipes require hot tap water.

All recipes have been developed to appeal visually to children, as well as to their taste buds. All recipes have been tested by children of the target age, and there is a balance of savoury and sweet dishes. *All By Myself* offers the child an opportunity to develop solo skills whilst the parent can be sure of the safety angle.

Against each recipe I have put an age capability guidance figure. This is only for guidance and some recipes for a 10-year-old can easily be prepared by a capable 7-year-old.

All the dishes are prepared by hand but with parents' permission electric toasters and kettles may be used, especially by older children.

The children who tested the recipes enjoyed making all the dishes and the adults enjoyed eating them even more.

For Children

It is fun to cook and make delicious things to eat for your brothers, sisters, mummy, daddy, grandparents, uncles, aunts and friends.

The wonderful thing about this cook book is that whatever you prepare from it will be SAFE. Adults will leave you in the kitchen to get on with your work without fussing. Surprise them by producing a super starter to a meal or, maybe, a pudding afterwards. Or ask if you can make lunch, tea or supper today.

There are also recipes for sweets which you can wrap prettily and give as presents. Everyone always appreciates a 'home made' present much more than one bought in a shop. Anyway, it usually tastes much nicer.

Every recipe has been given a suggested minimum age for making it. Remember this is only for guidance and some recipes for a 10-year-old can easily be prepared by a capable 7-year-old. And a recipe for a 4-year-old can be a super one for any age group to make.

Please read the *'Before you start'* section before you do anything else. Then, enjoy making the recipes as much as my children, their friends and I have done in preparing this book.

The equipment you need for preparing each recipe is in *italics*. Before beginning a recipe get all these items together so they are at hand.

When you have finished, remember to clean everything up. You must do it *all by yourself*!

Have fun.

USEFUL HINTS BEFORE YOU START

1 Read the recipe carefully.
2 Clean your work surface.
3 Make sure that you have all the ingredients in the house.
4 Collect all your equipment so that you don't have to stop in the middle of the recipe.
5 Wash your hands.
6 Put on an apron to protect your clothes.
7 If you have long hair, tie it back so that it does not get in your eyes.
8 After weighing out the ingredients you need, put the rest away.
9 If anything spills on the floor, mop it up straightaway to avoid accidents.
10 Keep your work surface clean and tidy so that you don't get in a mess.
11 Wash and dry all the equipment you have used.
12 After you finish, wash the working surface and sweep the floor.

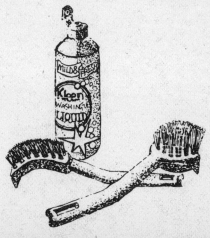

HOW TO MEASURE

All the quantities are given in Imperial/Metric measures. It is not always possible to calculate an exact equivalent but if you follow ONE TYPE of the measure, EITHER Imperial OR Metric throughout the recipe, you will be successful.

Make sure you know what a TABLESPOON, DESSERT-SPOON and a TEASPOON are.

IMPERIAL MEASURE = pound (lb)   ounce (oz)
                    inch (in)

METRIC MEASURE   = kilogram (kg)   gram (gr)
                    millilitre (ml) centimetre (cm)

AN AMERICAN CONVERSION TABLE

Almonds, ground	50gr/2 oz/4 heaped tablespoons
Baked beans, canned	450gr/15½ oz/1 tablespoon
Butter	15gr/½ oz/1 tablespoon
Cheese, cream	250gr/½ lb/1 cup
Cheese, grated	125gr/¼ lb/1 cup
Coconut, dessicated	125gr/¼ lb/1 cup (packed)
Crackers	250gr/8 oz/1½ cups
Cream	250ml/½ pint/1 cup
Fruit, fresh	500gr/1 lb (generous)/ 1 lb (generous)
Fruit, dried	250gr/½ lb/1½ cups
Honey	300gr/12 oz/1 cup
Milk, evaporated	200gr/7 fl oz/1 cup
Milk, condensed	200gr/7 fl oz/1 cup
Nuts, shelled	100gr/4 oz/1 cup
Oil	175ml/6 fl oz/1 cup
Peanut butter	250g/½ lb/under ½ cup
Raisins	250gr/½ lb/1½ cups
Rice Krispies	25g/1 oz/14 tablespoons
Salmon, can	225gr/7½ oz/1 cup
Sugar, caster (powdered)	100gr/4 oz/½ cup
Tomato juice, can (no. 2)	540ml/19 fl oz/2½ cups
Tuna, can	225gr/7½ oz/1 rounded cup
Vegetables, canned	225gr/7½ oz/1 rounded cup
Yogurt	250ml/½ pint/1 cup

BREAKFAST

Cowboys' Breakfast *(7 years)*

1 450g/15½ oz tin of baked beans
4 frankfurter sausages
1 teaspoon runny honey
½ teaspoon yellow french mustard
¼ teaspoon salt
pinch pepper
1 teaspoon Worcester sauce

1 With a *tin opener,* open the tin and pour the beans into *a pot.*
2 Cut up the frankfurters using *kitchen scissors* and add to the pot.
3 Add all other ingredients and mix with *a wooden spoon.*

You have enough breakfast to feed four cowboys.

Good For You Breakfast (8 years)

4 wholewheat cereal biscuits
2 tablespoons runny honey
2 eating apples
1 tablespoon lemon juice
2 bananas
1 tablespoon chopped nuts
1 tablespoon seedless raisins

1 With *a knife* thickly spread the biscuits with honey and place one in each of *four cereal bowls*.
2 Wash and dry the apples. Then grate them on *a grater*, throwing away the cores, and divide the grated apple between the bowls.
3 Sprinkle the contents of each bowl with lemon juice. With *a small knife* slice the peeled bananas and add them to the apples.
4 Add all other ingredients and enjoy your breakfast.

You can pour some milk on the top or yogurt or cream if you like.

Some children like this breakfast served as a pudding after dinner.

SOUP

Cucumber and Yogurt Soup *(9 years)*

½ thin cucumber
1 small clove of garlic
300ml/½ pint plain yogurt
2 teaspoons caster sugar
2 teaspoons lemon juice
1 teaspoon salt
½ teaspoon white pepper

1 With *a peeler* peel the cucumber and then grate it on *a grater* into *a large bowl*.
2 Peel the skin from a clove of garlic and place in *a garlic squeezer* and squeeze into the bowl.
3 Add the yogurt, sugar, lemon juice, salt and pepper. Mix with *a fork* and place in the fridge.

This soup is delicious on a hot summer's day and it must be served very cold.

Cold Tomato Soup *(9 years)*

1 540ml/19 fl oz tin of tomato juice
1 orange
¼ cucumber
1 firm tomato
1 small onion
1 teaspoon Worcester sauce (2 if you like it HOT)
4 drops tabasco sauce (7 if you like it HOT)
½ teaspoon salt
¼ teaspoon pepper
1 clove of garlic

1 With *a tin opener* open the tin of tomato juice and pour it into *a large bowl*.
2 Place the orange on *a chopping board* and, with *a knife*, cut it in half. Squeeze out the juice on *a squeezer* and add to the tomato juice.
3 With *a peeler* peel the cucumber and with *a knife* cut it lengthways into four long pieces. Then cut it across into cubes. Add these to the juices.
4 Wash the tomato. Place on the chopping board and with *a knife* cut into quarters. Cut away the core and chop the rest into small pieces. Add to the bowl.
5 Peel the onion and grate using *a grater*. Add a *teaspoonful* of the grated onion to the soup.
6 Add the Worcester sauce, tabasco, salt and pepper.
7 Peel the clove of garlic and place in *a garlic squeezer*. Squeeze into the bowl.
8 Mix it all together and place the bowl in the fridge.

You will have enough for four people.

Creamy Avocado Soup *(9 years +)*

2 ripe avocados
1 teaspoon lemon juice
1 420g/15 oz tin of consommé soup
300ml/½ pint plain yogurt
150ml/¼ pint bottle tomato juice
½ teaspoon salt
¼ teaspoon white pepper
3 drops tabasco sauce
150ml/¼ pint double cream
small bunch of chives

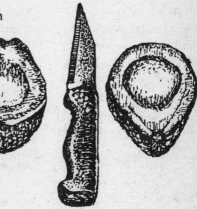

1 Place the avocados on *a chopping board* and, using *a knife*, cut in half lengthwise. Remove the stones. With *a spoon* remove the flesh and sprinkle with lemon juice.
2 With *a wooden spoon* rub the avocado flesh through *a nylon sieve* into *a large bowl*.
3 With *a tin opener* open the tin of consommé and add to the bowl.
4 Pour in the yogurt, tomato juice and tabasco sauce and add the salt and pepper.
5 Place the double cream in another *bowl* and whisk lightly with *a whisk* until slightly thickened. Add to the bowl containing the other ingredients.
6 Mix everything until blended.
7 With *kitchen scissors* snip some chives into the bowl and place the soup in the fridge until you are ready to eat it.

FISHY DISHES

Devilled Tunny Fish *(9 years)*

1 210g/7½ oz tin of tunny fish in brine
1 tablespoon white wine vinegar
2 tablespoons tomato ketchup
1 teaspoon yellow french mustard
3 tablespoons corn oil
pinch of salt
pinch of pepper
410g/14 oz tin french beans
cayenne pepper
1 small red pepper
6 black or green olives

1 With *a tin opener* open the tin of tunny fish and drain off the liquid.
2 In *a bowl* mix the vinegar, tomato ketchup, mustard, oil, salt and pepper and whisk with *a fork*.
3 Add the tunny fish and mix with *a spoon* so that the fish is well coated with the dressing.
4 With the tin opener open the tin of french beans. Drain away the liquid.
5 Place the french beans on the bottom of *an oval serving dish*. Spoon the tuna mixture along the middle so that the green beans are visible on each side. Sprinkle some cayenne pepper on the fish.
6 Wash the red pepper and place it on *a chopping board*. Cut in half with *a knife* and throw away all the pips. Slice thinly into strips.
7 Arrange the pepper strips and olives in a lattice pattern on the top.

Kipper Paté (7 years)

1 200g/7 oz tin of kippers in vegetable oil
6 teaspoons lemon juice
150g/4 oz cream cheese
freshly ground black pepper
sprig of parsley
1 slice of lemon

1 Open the tin of kippers and, with *a fork*, remove the fish, leaving the oil behind. Throw away the tin and vegetable oil.
2 Place the kippers in *a bowl* and, with the fork, mash till pretty smooth.
3 Add the lemon juice and mash again. Continue mashing while you add the cheese.
4 Turn *the pepper grinder* six times over the kipper mixture.
5 Place in *a paté dish*. Add a sprig of parsley and a slice of lemon on top and eat with hot toast or crunchy bread.

The lemon juice sometimes runs to the bottom of the pate. Just stir again before serving.

Sardine Tomatoes *(9 years)*

4 large or 6 small tomatoes
1 tin of sardines in oil
2 tablespoons curd or cream cheese
2 teaspoons lemon juice
¼ teaspoon cayenne pepper
pinch of white pepper
¼ teaspoon salt
handful of parsley
4 or 6 lettuce leaves

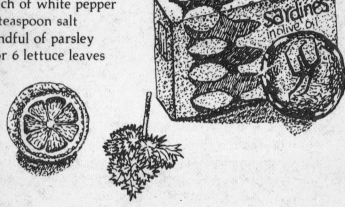

1 Wash the tomatoes. With *a knife* cut off the tops.
2 With *a teaspoon* scoop out the seeds and flesh. Put the tomato cases and tops aside and throw the insides away.
3 With *a tin opener* open the tin of sardines.
4 With *a fork* remove the sardines on to *a plate*.
5 With *a knife and fork* cut down the back of each sardine and remove the backbone.
6 Mash the flesh with the same fork and put it in *a bowl* with the cheese, lemon juice, salt, pepper and cayenne pepper. Mix everything together.
7 Wash a handful of parsley and shake it dry. Pick off the curly leaves and place them in *a mug*.
8 Holding *the kitchen scissors* in the mug, chop the parsley very finely.
9 Mix the parsley with the sardine mixture.
10 Fill the tomato cases and replace the tops, slanting them slightly. Add a sprig of parsley and place each tomato on a lettuce leaf.

Salmon Oyster Shells *(10 years)*

juice from one lemon
2 teaspoons gelatine
2 tablespoons hot water
1 213g/7 oz tin of pink salmon
4 tablespoons thick mayonnaise
125ml/¼ pint double cream
¼ cucumber
pinch of salt
pinch of pepper
8 bridge rolls
8 washed lettuce leaves

1 Place the lemon on *a chopping board* and, with *a knife*, cut it in half. Squeeze out the juice from each half with *a lemon squeezer*.
2 Put the gelatine into *a cup*.
3 Add two *tablespoons* of hot tap water and the lemon juice to the gelatine.* (See below.)
4 With *a fork* whisk until the gelatine has melted and looks clear. Stand the cup in *a bowl* of hot tap water.
5 With *a tin opener* open the tin of salmon.
6 Carefully drain away the liquid and place the salmon on *a large plate*.
7 Mash with *a fork*, discarding any black skin and hard little bones.
8 Add the mayonnaise and mix with the fork.
9 Pour the cream into *a biggish basin* and whisk with *a fork* until thicker but still runny.
10 Peel the cucumber with *a peeler* and, on *a grater*, grate into the cream.
11 Add the melted gelatine and the salmon mixture to the cream and mix together. Season with salt and pepper. Place in a fridge.

12 With *a knife* cut the rolls almost right through and scoop out the white or brown bread in the middle, turning the rolls into shells.

13 Take the mousse out of the fridge and, with *a spoon*, fill the 'oyster shells' with it.

14 Place each 'shell' on a lettuce leaf on *a plate*.

* If your hot tap water is not safe for drinking, boil *an electric kettle* and let it stand for two minutes before you pour two tablespoons of water on to the gelatine.

Smoked Mackerel and Potato Dish

(10 years)

2 smoked mackerels
1 egg
3 teaspoons lemon juice
½ teaspoon strong french yellow mustard
1 teaspoon caster sugar
pinch of salt
pinch of pepper
125ml/¼ pint olive oil or corn oil
1 400g/14½ oz tin of new potatoes
1 spring onion
6 sprigs parsley

1 Place the fish on *a plate*. With *a fork* and *a knife* flake away the flesh from the skin removing any bones you may find.
2 Place the flaked fish in *a dish*.
3 Prepare *a mixing bowl* and *a cup*. Crack the egg against the cup and carefully break the shell, letting the white of the egg slide out into the cup and putting the yolk into the bowl.
4 To the yolk, add the lemon juice, mustard, sugar, salt and pepper. Mix well with *a fork*. Gradually add the oil, beating all the time.
5 With *a tin opener*, open the tin of potatoes and drain away the liquid. On *a chopping board*, cut the potatoes into quarters and add them to the fish.
6 Wash the spring onion. With *a knife* cut away the bottom and some of the tough green leaves. Slice the rest thinly and add to the dish.
7 Gently mix in the sauce and, with *kitchen scissors*, chop the parsley and scatter on top. Eat with crunchy brown bread.

Tuna Tomatoes (9 years)

6 tomatoes
1 225g/7½ oz tin of tuna fish in vegetable oil
2 tablespoons mayonnaise
freshly ground black pepper
6 sprigs parsley

1 Wash the tomatoes. With *a knife* cut off the tops.
2 With *a teaspoon* scoop out the seeds and flesh. Put the tomato cases and tops aside and throw away the insides.
3 With *a tin opener* open the tin of tuna.
4 With *a fork* remove the tuna and oil on to *a deep plate*.
5 Mash the tuna with the fork until quite smooth.
6 Add the mayonnaise and turn the black *pepper grinder* 6 times over the tuna and mayonnaise mixture. Mix well.
7 Using *a teaspoon*, fill the empty tomato cases with the tuna mixture.
8 Replace the tops, slanting them slightly. Add a sprig of parsley on the top.

These tuna tomatoes will make a delicious starter to a main meal. Make them in advance and keep them in the fridge until you are ready to serve them. Some wholemeal bread and butter would be lovely to have with them.

Sardine Salad *(10 years)*

1 round lettuce
2 tomatoes
1 small onion
1 tin of sardines
french dressing (see page 28)
1 lemon

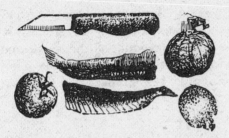

1 Wash the lettuce, discarding any outside leaves which are wilted and brown at the edges. Dry the rest in *a salad drier* and wrap the lettuce in *a clean tea towel*. Place in the fridge to crispen.
2 Wash and dry the tomatoes, place them on *a chopping board* and slice with *a knife*.
3 Peel the skin from the onion and slice the onion thinly with the knife.
4 Open the tin of sardines with *a tin opener*.
5 Take the lettuce out of the fridge and with your hands break it up into small pieces. Place on *four plates* or *one long dish*.
6 Drain away the oil from the sardines and place the fish on top of the lettuce.
7 Arrange the tomato slices and the onion slices round the sardines and make the french dressing.
8 Cut the lemon into 4 and place each quarter on the side of one plate.

Eat the salad with lots of buttered brown bread and squeeze the lemon quarters over the sardines.

French Dressing

1 teaspoon french yellow mustard
1 teaspoon caster sugar
juice from ½ lemon
½ teaspoon salt
¼ teaspoon ground white pepper
200ml/7 fl oz oil

Place all the ingredients in *a jug* and beat with *a fork* until smooth. You will need about half the above amount for the sardine salad. The rest will keep in the fridge for a month or even longer but must be well covered or placed in a screw top jar.

PICK ME UPS

Little Green Balls *(8 years)*

25g/1 oz cooked chicken
50g/2 oz cream cheese
15g/½ oz crunchy peanut butter
1 dessertspoon mayonnaise
bunch of parsley

1 Weigh the chicken on *the kitchen scales* and place on *a chopping board*.
2 With *a fork* and *a knife*, cut up chicken into tiny pieces or use a *hand mincer* and mince it. Place in *a mixing bowl*.
3 Add the peanut butter, mayonnaise and the cream cheese. Mix well with *a wooden spoon*.
4 Divide the mixture into eight parts and, with fingers, roll into balls.
5 To chop the parsley, place the washed sprigs in *a mug* and, with *kitchen scissors*, chop until fine.
6 Place the parsley on *a plate* and roll each ball in it. Leave in a fridge for half an hour to firm a little.

Blue Paté (8 years)

125g/5 oz blue cheese
100g/4 oz curd cheese
1 small onion
2 pinches cayenne pepper
1 teaspoon Worcester sauce
chives
savoury crackers

1 Weigh the cheeses on *the kitchen scales*.
2 Place the curd cheese in *a large mixing bowl*.
3 With *a grater*, grate the blue cheese into the bowl.
4 Peel the onion and grate about a teaspoonful into the cheeses in the bowl.
5 Add two pinches of cayenne pepper and the Worcester sauce. With *a wooden spoon*, mix very well. With *kitchen scissors* snip some chives on top.
6 Place the paté in *a little dish* or spread on the savoury crackers.

Grown-ups enjoy this very much with drinks or as a savoury instead of pudding.

Kebabs *(8 years)*

wooden skewers or cocktail sticks
250g/8 oz cooked garlic sausage in one piece
4 carrots
1 bunch radishes
½ cucumber
50g/2 oz cheese such as cheddar or edam
1 cabbage or grapefruit for presentation (not essential)

1 Skin the sausage and place on *a chopping board*. With *a knife* slice thickly into 5 or 6 slices and then cut into cubes.
2 With *a peeler* peel the carrots and wash them. Trim off the top and bottom and slice the carrots thickly.
3 Wash the radishes, trim off the ends, and if the radishes are very big slice them or cut them in half.
4 Wash the cucumber and slice thickly. Half or quarter each slice.
5 Cut the cheese into bite-size pieces.
6 Thread the different pieces of food – they should be more or less the same size – on to the skewers or cocktail sticks.
7 If you like, you can stick your kebabs into a cabbage or a grapefruit so that everyone can help themselves.
8 To eat – using *a fork* remove the chunks of food from the skewers.

It's lovely to have kebabs at a tea party. They look terrific and taste even better.

Cucumber Castles *(10 years)*

1 slim straight cucumber
100g/4 oz peeled prawns *or* a small tin of crabmeat, salmon or
  tuna
2 stalks celery
1 tablespoon mayonnaise
1 bunch watercress

1 Wash the cucumber and dry it.
2 Using *a peeler*, peel lengthwise alternate strips of
   cucumber skin to give a striped effect. This will be about
   five stripes. Trim a small slice off each end of cucumber
   with *a knife*.
3 Now cut the cucumber into 2½ cm/1 inch lengths.
4 With *a small teaspoon*, scoop out just one spoonful of
   cucumber seeds from each length so that a cup is formed
   at one end.
5 Stand the cucumber castles on *a plate* and place in the
   refrigerator.
6 On *a chopping board* roughly chop the prawns, *or* with *a tin
   opener*, open the tin of crabmeat, salmon or tuna and drain
   away any liquid.
7 Place the fish (prawns, crabmeat, salmon or tuna) in *a
   mixing bowl*.
8 Scrub and wash the celery and, with *a knife* or *a chopper*
   finely chop and add to the fish mixture. Mix in the
   mayonnaise.
9 Heap spoonfuls of the mixture into the scooped-out holes
   in the 'castles'.
10 Wash and shake the watercress. Using *kitchen scissors* trim
   away the stalks and place the watercress in the middle of *a
   dish*. Surround with the 'castles'. There should be about
   twelve.

Ham Wrappers (9 years)

1 crisp eating apple
125g/4 oz cream cheese
4 slices of ham
24 wooden cocktail sticks

1 Place the apple on *a chopping board*. Quarter, core and slice each piece into six slices using *a knife*.
2 Spread the cream cheese on each slice.
3 Place the four slices of ham on a board and cut in half lengthwise and then across into three sections. You should have 24 pieces of ham.
4 Wrap each piece of ham round a piece of apple. Secure with a cocktail stick.

It's a lovely thing to make for a party. Eat as soon as you can so that the apple stays crisp.

Celery Boats (9 years)

1 small head of celery
50g/2 oz walnuts
175g/6 oz cream cheese
freshly ground black pepper
large pinch of salt
1 tablespoon milk

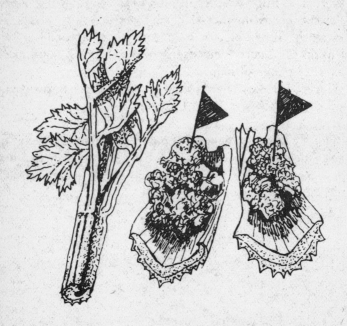

1 With *a knife*, trim the ends of the stalks of celery and scrub each one well.
2 On *a chopping board* cut celery into 5 cm/2 inch lengths.
3 Place the walnuts in *a small plastic bag* and crush them with *a rolling pin*.
4 Place the nuts, cheese, pepper, salt and milk in *a bowl*. Mix with *a wooden spoon*.
5 Fill the celery boats with the mixture using *a teaspoon*.

Pinwheel Sandwiches (10 years)

1 square edged loaf of bread (unsliced)
softened butter or margarine
various spreads eg. sliced ham, soft cheese, marmite, jam, peanut butter etc.
few parsley sprigs

1 Take the loaf of bread and stand it on its end on *a bread board*.
2 With *a bread knife* carefully slice off the top crust and carry on slicing the rest of the loaf lengthwise as thinly as possible.
3 Cut off the crusts. Place each slice on a flat working surface and with *a rolling pin* roll out to make it thin and supple.
4 Spread each slice with butter or margarine using *a knife*.
5 Either cover some of the slices with ham or spread with various spreads you have chosen.
6 Starting at one end, roll them up carefully.
7 Wrap the rolls in *foil* and place in the fridge for half an hour.
8 Remove the foil and slice each roll into rounds with *a knife*.
9 Place the pinwheels on *a dish* and cover until ready to eat. Add a few parsley sprigs to add more colour.

Pinwheels look very professional and are often served in hotels and restaurants with drinks. I think they look pretty and are fun to make.

Checkerboard of Sandwiches *(7 years)*

6 slices of brown bread
6 slices of white bread
softened butter or soft margarine
various savoury spreads eg. yellow cheese, white creamy
   cheese, cucumber, ham, thin slices of salami (skin
   removed), thin slices chicken, turkey, beef etc.
parsley sprigs or mustard and cress

1 Place each slice of bread on *a bread board* and with *a knife* cut
   off the crusts.
2 Spread each slice with butter or margarine.
3 Spread or place various toppings on each slice and then cut
   each one into 4 squares.
4 Arrange the squares on *a tray* side by side, contrasting
   colours next to each other like a checkerboard. Eg. yellow
   cheese, white cheese, ham, cucumber, chicken and salami
   at the top and the next row could be: cucumber, salami,
   yellow cheese, ham, white cheese, chicken.
5 Surround with a border of parsley sprigs or mustard and
   cress.
6 Cover with cling film until you are ready to serve or eat
   them.

You could use sweet spreads eg. cheese mixed with apricot or
other jam, lemon curd, peanut butter, lime jelly, marmalade
etc. and have a sweet checkerboard of sandwiches.

Bread Pictures (5 years)

10 slices white or brown bread
softened butter or margarine
10 slices ham or corned beef
5 slices processed cheese
'animal' biscuit cutters

1 With *a knife* spread the butter or margarine on the bread
  slices.
2 Lay the slices of ham or beef on the bread.
3 With *the 'animal' biscuit cutters*, cut out the middle of each slice
  of cheese.
4 Place the five cheese animal-shapes on five pieces of the
  ham/corned beef sandwiches and the five cheese-frames
  on the other five sandwiches.

If you are five or six years old then you can make these fun
sandwiches for your friends. If you have very young brothers
or sisters you could prepare these animal pictures for their
tea or birthday party and see how they love them.

Dips with Crudites *(8 years)*

Crudites are raw vegetables

Crudites
4 carrots
4 sticks celery
1 red pepper
1 small cauliflower
1 bunch radishes
1 fennel bulb
Choose vegetables you enjoy eating raw.

1 Using *a peeler* peel the carrots. Trim them with *a knife* and cut into sticks. Place in *a bowl* of cold water.
2 Wash, scrub and trim the celery with the knife and cut into sticks. Place in *a bowl* of cold water.
3 Wash the pepper. Place on *a chopping board* and cut in half with the knife. Remove all the pips and cut into pieces about 6 cm/2½ inches long. Place in *a small polythene bag*.
4 Remove any leaves from the outside of the cauliflower. Break off all the separate 'florets' of the cauliflower and wash them. Place in the bowl of cold water.

5 Remove any brown outside pieces from the fennel bulb. Wash the rest. With the knife trim and cut into bite size pieces. Place in a bowl of cold water.
6 Trim the radishes, leaving some of the green. Wash and place in the bowl of cold water.
7 Place all the prepared vegetables in the fridge. Now make the dips. You don't have to make them all. Just choose the ones that appeal to you most.

Herb Dip
250g/½ lb curd cheese
125ml/4 fl oz double cream
1 tablespoon chopped chives
1 tablespoon chopped parsley
½ teaspoon salt
¼ teaspoon pepper
1 tablespoon mixed, chopped herbs (eg. marjoram, taragon, thyme, dill)

1 Mix everything, in *a mixing bowl*, using *a wooden spoon*.
2 Pile the mixture in the middle of *a large plate or dish*.
3 Surround mixture with the raw vegetables which you have taken out of the fridge and drained.

Tomato Dip
250g/½ lb cream cheese
6 tablespoons tomato ketchup

1 Place the cream cheese in *a bowl* and, with *a fork*, beat in the ketchup.
2 Place the bowl on a *large plate* or *round tray* and surround the bowl with the raw vegetables which you have taken out of the fridge and drained.

Secret Dip
150ml/¼pt double cream
150ml/¼pt mayonnaise

1 Place the double cream and mayonnaise in *a large bowl* and, using *a whisk,* whisk until thick.

Nobody can ever guess what the secret dip mixture is. You can keep it a secret!

Also, remember that crackers and crisps are good for dips.

Ham Soldiers *(9 years)*

75g/3 oz ham
½ teaspoon cayenne pepper
½ teaspoon French mustard
15g/½ oz butter
1 tablespoon Worcester sauce
1 tablespoon tomato ketchup
6 slices bread or toast

1 Place the ham on *a chopping board* and, with *a fork and a knife,* cut up very finely or mince in *a hand mincer.*
2 Place the ham in *a bowl* and add all other ingredients except the bread. Mix with *a wooden spoon.*
3 If you are allowed to use *a toaster,* toast the bread.
4 With *a knife* spread the ham mixture on the bread or toast.
5 Place the bread/toast on *a breadboard* and cut off the crusts. Cut into 'soldiers' and arrange on *a plate.*

MEALS IN A HURRY

Club Sandwich *(9 years)*

3 slices of white bread
softened butter or margarine
1 firm tomato (sliced)
2 lettuce leaves (washed and dried)
2 slices of cooked chicken or turkey
4 slices of cucumber
2 tablespoons mayonnaise
2 olives, stoned
2 cocktail sticks

1 In *an electric toaster* toast the bread and with *a knife* cut off the crusts.
2 Spread the butter or margarine on one side of two pieces of toast and on both sides of the third piece.
3 Cover 2 slices (one with both sides buttered and another) with slices of tomato and cucumber, chicken or turkey, lettuce and mayonnaise. Carefully place the slice with both sides buttered on top of the other one and press together.
4 Press the third piece of toast firmly on the top, butter side down, and with *a bread knife* cut in two.
5 Spear each club sandwich with a cocktail stick and place a stoned olive on top. Eat with a knife and fork.

Club sandwich is an American invention and is getting more and more popular in England. It makes a wonderfully delicious and wholesome snack when there is no time to have a cooked meal. It is just the thing to enjoy in front of the TV. Try one of the milkshakes at the end of this book with it.

Double Decker *(8 years)*

3 slices of your favourite bread
softened butter or margarine
2 slices cheese or ham
2 teaspoons chutney or mayonnaise
2 washed lettuce leaves
1 firm tomato (sliced)

1 With *a knife* spread 2 slices of bread on one side with butter
  or margarine and the third slice on both sides.
2 Place the cheese or ham on top of only two slices (one with
  both sides buttered and another). Spread with chutney or
  mayonnaise.
3 Top with lettuce and sliced tomato. Place the slice with
  both sides buttered on top of the other and press together.
4 Place the third slice of bread on top, buttered side down.
  Cut in half with *a bread knife*. Place on *a plate* and serve.

Triple Decker *(9 years)*

4 slices of brown or white bread
softened butter or margarine
3 lettuce leaves, washed and dried
3 teaspoons mayonnaise
1 225g/7½ oz tin of tuna fish
freshly ground black pepper
1 small onion
6 slices of cucumber
2 cocktail sticks

1 Using *a knife* spread the slices of bread with butter or margarine. On three buttered slices, place a lettuce leaf. Spread with mayonnaise.

2 With *a tin opener* open the tin of tuna and drain away the oil or liquid.

3 Divide the tuna between the three slices. Grind some black pepper on top.

4 Place the onion on *a chopping board* and, with *a knife*, trim, peel and slice thinly.

5 Place the onion slices on top of the tuna. Add the cucumber slices on top of that and pile the 3 slices of bread on top of each other. Place the last slice of bread, buttered side down, on the very top.

6 Cut in half using *a bread knife*. Spear each half with a cocktail stick to keep it in place. Eat with a knife and fork.

Pitta Pockets *(6 years)*

pitta bread
softened butter or margarine
slices of cold meat eg. chicken, beef, ham, lamb, pork etc.
sliced cheese, such as cheddar
cucumber slices
onion rings
sliced tomato
washed and dried lettuce leaves
mayonnaise or chutney

1 Place the pitta on *a chopping board* and with *a knife*, cut across in half. Separate with your fingers to form two pockets.
2 Spread the insides with butter or margarine. Stuff as much of the above ingredients into the pockets as you wish. Add some mayonnaise or chutney and eat in your fingers.

Pitta pockets are always very popular and are great fun to make for a picnic. Everyone can choose their favourite filling.

Traffic Light Sandwiches *(10 years)*

My 12 year old daughter, Victoria, made these for the book

2 slices of white bread
softened butter or margarine
1 slice of ham
1 tablespoon tomato ketchup
1 tablespoon thousand island dressing
1 tablespoon mayonnaise mixed with 1 tablespoon chopped
  parsley or chives

1 Using *a knife*, spread the butter or margarine on one of the
  pieces of bread.
2 Place the ham on top of the buttered piece.
3 Imagine that the slice with ham is divided lengthwise into
  three equal sections. Evenly spread tomato ketchup on the
  left section. Spread the middle section with thousand
  island dressing and the right with green mayonnaise.
4 Place the unbuttered slice of bread next to the coloured one
  and with the back of *a knife* divide into the same sections,
  but do not cut.
5 With your finger make two holes in each section, one
  above the other.
6 Place the slice of bread on top of the coloured piece and
  press down gently. You will have 2 red holes, 2 orange
  holes and 2 green holes.
7 Now cut the sandwich sideways in two and you have 2
  traffic light sandwiches.

You can also use tomatoes for the red light, grated carrot for
orange and a lettuce leaf for the green lights.

Jumbo Sandwich *(10 years)*

1 small french stick
softened butter or margarine
2 tablespoons cream cheese or grated cheese
1 tablespoon chopped chives or spring onions
6 thin slices of salami or continental type of sausage
2 sliced tomatoes
3 lettuce leaves, washed and dried

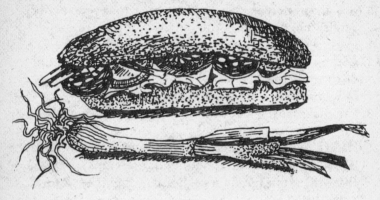

1 Using *a bread knife*, cut the loaf lengthwise in half.
2 With your hands, hollow out the bottom half of the bread.
3 Spread both sides with softened butter or margarine.
4 Spread the hollowed half with cheese. Add the chives or
   spring onions.
5 Remove the skin from salami or sausage (if there is any)
   and place the slices on top of the cheese.
6 Top with lettuce leaves and then with sliced tomatoes.
   Cover with the other half of the bread. Cut the jumbo
   sandwich in half. There is enough for two of you.

Use the bread you took out of the hollow to feed the birds and
ducks. They love it.

Sweet and Sour Ham Parcels (8 years)

100g/4 oz cream cheese
2 tablespoons yogurt (plain)
¼ teaspoon salt
pinch pepper
2 tablespoons tinned sweet corn
5 or 6 slices thinly sliced ham
tinned pineapple chunks
5 or 6 lettuce leaves

1 Place the cheese, yogurt, salt and pepper in *a mixing bowl* and, with *a fork*, beat until smooth.
2 With *a tin opener* open the tin of sweet corn and add 2 *tablespoons* to the cheese mixture.
3 Divide the mixture between the slices of ham with *a teaspoon* and roll the slices up.
4 Place a pineapple chunk at each end of the ham parcel.
5 Wash and dry the lettuce leaves. Spread on *a serving dish* or *plates* and serve the ham parcels on top of the lettuce.

SALADS AND OTHER DISHES

Chicken, Tuna and Nuts *(10 years)*

1 lettuce
4 sticks of celery or 1 fennel bulb
1 212g/7½ oz tin of tuna fish in oil
225g/8 oz cold cooked chicken
1 handful of nuts such as peanuts, cashews or almonds
1 egg yolk
1 teaspoon french yellow mustard
1 teaspoon salt
½ teaspoon ground pepper
juice from ½ lemon
2 tablespoons olive oil
small bunch of parsley

1 Wash the lettuce, discarding any withered and brown leaves. Shake dry. Tear into smallish pieces with your hands and place in *a salad bowl or a serving dish*.
2 Scrub the celery or wash the fennel bulb, discarding any brown outside pieces. Trim with *a knife* and slice on *a chopping board*. Add to the bowl.
3 With *a tin opener* open the tin of tuna. Pour the oil into *a jug* and keep it for making the mayonnaise.
4 Break up the tuna with *a fork* and add to the bowl.
5 With your hands, break up the chicken and add it together with the nuts to the bowl.
6 Now make the mayonnaise. Crack the egg against *a cup* and separate the white from the yolk. Let the egg white trickle out into the cup and keep it for another recipe (maybe to make apple snow). Add the yolk to the jug of oil from the tuna. Add the mustard, salt, pepper, lemon juice and

gradually add the olive oil beating with *a fork* until the sauce is smooth. Pour over the salad.

7 With *kitchen scissors* snip some clean parsley on top.

This is quite a filling salad and can be served as a main course for lunch or supper for the whole family.

Healthnut Salad *(10 years)*

1 round lettuce
1 small ripe melon
3 nectarines
18 black cherries
12 strawberries
6 teaspoons sunflower oil
12 teaspoons orange juice
6 teaspoons lemon juice
3 teaspoons runny honey
pinch salt
6 teaspoons natural sunflower seeds
few parsley sprigs

1 Take the lettuce and throw away any yellow or withered outside leaves. Wash the rest leaf by leaf. Dry in *a salad drier* or shake dry and place in *a salad bowl*.
2 With *a knife* cut the melon in half. Use *a spoon* to remove the seeds. Throw them away.
3 With *a dessertspoon* remove the flesh from the melon and place in the salad bowl.
4 Wash the nectarines. Cut in half with *a knife* and remove the stones. Slice the nectarines and add to the bowl.

5 Wash the cherries and with your fingers remove the stones and stalks. Add the cherries to the salad.

6 Remove the green tops from the strawberries and add the berries to the other fruit.

7 In *a cup* mix the oil, orange and lemon juice, honey and salt. Using *a fork* beat until the sauce is smooth and pour over the salad.

8 Scatter the sunflower seeds over the top and place the parsley sprigs round the edge inside the bowl.

Stuffed Cabbage Salad *(11 years)*

700g/1½ lb cabbage
2 eating apples
125g/4 oz cold roast pork (sliced)
2 tablespoons olive oil
½ teaspoon french yellow mustard
large pinch salt
pinch white pepper
2 tablespoons sweet cider
2 tablespoons sour cream
handful of parsley

1 Place the cabbage on *a chopping board* and using *a knife* cut off the bottom. Remove all the yellow and withered outside leaves.
2 Break off some large leaves and wash and dry them. Use them for lining the inside of *a large bowl*. Put the lined bowl in a cool place.
3 Wash the rest of the cabbage and place on a chopping board. Slice as thinly as possible and add to the lined bowl.
4 With *a peeler* peel the apples. Take out the core with *a knife* and slice the apples. With *a knife and fork* cut up the slices of pork and, together with the apple, add to the cabbage.
5 Put the oil into *a jug*. Add the mustard, salt, pepper, cider and cream and beat with *a fork* until smooth. Pour over the salad.
6 Wash the parsley, shake dry and with *kitchen scissors* cut the leaves into the bowl. Throw away the stalks.

Chef's Salad *(9 years)*

1 cos, webb or round lettuce
1 kabanos or peperami
2 firm tomatoes
1 very small tin of pineapple chunks
175g/6 oz cooked chicken
1 bunch parsley
3 tablespoons olive oil
½ teaspoon french yellow mustard
1 teaspoon caster sugar
2 teaspoons lemon juice
large pinch salt
large pinch pepper

1 Discard any yellow or withered leaves from the lettuce and wash the rest leaf by leaf. Shake dry or dry in *a salad drier*. Place in *a large salad bowl*.
2 Place the peperami on *a chopping board* and slice with *a knife*. If using kabanos, remove the skin before slicing.
3 Wash the tomatoes, quarter and remove the cores. Add to the salad.
4 Open the tin of pineapple chunks with *a tin opener*. Drain the juice from the pineapple chunks before adding them to the salad.
5 On *the kitchen scales* weigh the chicken and break up into bite size pieces using your hands. Remove the skin before adding to the salad.
6 Wash the parsley and, with *kitchen scissors*, cut off the leaves from the parsley stalks and add the leaves to the salad.
7 Now make the dressing. Put the oil into *a jug* and add the lemon juice, mustard, salt, pepper and sugar. Mix and beat with *a fork* until smooth. Pour over the salad just before you eat it.

As this is a chef's salad and *you* are the chef, you can add other types of meat or vegetables or fruit you enjoy to eat. I think that adding sweet corn, cucumber and onions could be delicious, but I leave it for you to decide.

Beef À La Française *(10 years)*

225g/8 oz cooked sliced beef
½ teaspoon french yellow mustard
1 teaspoon paprika pepper
pinch garlic salt
pinch salt
½ teaspoon caster sugar
juice from ½ lemon
3 tablespoons olive oil
2 large tomatoes
3 gherkins
6 slices of french bread
few parsley sprigs

1 Place the beef slices on *a chopping board* and with *a knife* cut them into strips.
2 In *a mixing bowl* using *a whisk,* whisk the mustard, paprika, garlic salt, salt, sugar, lemon juice and oil until smooth.
3 Add the strips of beef to the dressing. Stir round with *a wooden spoon* to make sure that every strip is coated with the sauce.
4 Wash the tomatoes. Place them on a chopping board and cut in half with *a knife.* Remove the hard cores and slice the rest.
5 Cut the gherkins in half. With *a small knife* cut the rounded ends into fan shapes.
6 Place the bread slices on *a flat dish.* Divide the beef mixture between the slices, piling it on top. Cover with tomato slices and place a gerkin fan on each slice. Place the parsley sprigs round the dish.

This is a special dish to prepare for your family and friends.

Chinese Salad *(9 years)*

1 bunch watercress
1 bunch radishes
2 sticks celery
2 carrots
1 bunch spring onions
3 tablespoons oil
2 teaspoons soya sauce
3 teaspoons lemon juice
2 teaspoons runny honey
pinch pepper

1 With *a knife*, cut the stalks from the watercress and wash the leaves. Dry in *a salad drier* and place in *a salad bowl*.
2 Trim and wash the radishes. With the knife carefully pare down red skins into petals. Place in *a bowl* of cold water.
3 Scrub the celery and trim with the knife. Cut into strips lengthwise and then into 4cm/1½ inch lengths.

4 Peel the carrots with *a peeler*. Trim, wash and slice with the knife.

5 With the knife trim the roots off the spring onions. Cut off the tops leaving about 5cm/2 inches. Wash and make cuts in the white bulbs. Place in the salad bowl white part uppermost.

6 Take the radishes out of the water, add to the salad bowl, together with the celery and the carrots.

7 Place the oil, soya sauce, lemon juice, honey and pepper in *a jug* and whisk with *a fork*. Pour the dressing over the salad.

Try using *chopsticks* to eat this pretty salad.

Russian Salad *(7 years)*

1 225g/7½ oz tin petit pois
1 225g/7½ oz tin new potatoes
1 225g/7½ oz tin baby carrots
1 225g/7½ oz tin broad beans
1 cooked beetroot
300ml/½ pint sour cream *or* thick set yogurt
handful chopped dill *or* parsley

1 With *a tin opener* open all the tins. Drain all the tinned vegetables in *a colander*.
2 Peel the skin from the beetroot. Place the beetroot on a chopping board and with *a knife* slice it, then cut it across and across again into small chunks.
3 Place all the vegetables in *a salad bowl*.
4 Pour the sour cream or yogurt over the vegetables and mix lightly with *a spoon*.
5 Using *the kitchen scissors* cut some dill or parsley over the salad.

You can make this salad a few hours before you eat it. Just cover the top with cling film and place in the fridge.

In Russia people eat brown rye bread with their meals. You could get some and enjoy eating your salad 'the Russian way'. Russian children drink buttermilk. If you've never tasted it, try some. It's creamy, refreshing and delicious.

Jamaican Salad *(8 years)*

1 lettuce
4 slices ham
2 bananas
2 teaspoons lemon juice
2 fresh or tinned apricots
150ml/¼ pint single cream
1 teaspoon caster sugar
½ teaspoon salt
¼ teaspoon white pepper
small bunch of parsley

1 Remove the yellow and withered outside leaves of the lettuce and wash the rest leaf by leaf. Shake dry.
2 Arrange the lettuce on *four plates* and place the slices of ham on top.
3 With *a knife*, thickly slice the peeled bananas. Arrange on top of the ham. Sprinkle with lemon juice.
4 Cut the apricots in half and remove the stones. Place each apricot half in the centre of the banana slices.
5 In *a cup* mix the cream, sugar, salt and pepper using *a fork* and carefully pour over each salad.
6 Arrange a few washed parsley sprigs round the edge of each plate.

Greek Salad *(8 years)*

1 lettuce
1 small onion
2 firm tomatoes
½ cucumber
125g/4 oz Feta cheese
2 teaspoonsful fresh basil
16 black olives (optional)
3 tablespoons good olive oil
½ teaspoon yellow Dijon mustard
juice from ½ lemon
½ teaspoon salt
¼ teaspoon freshly ground black pepper

1 Remove the yellow and withered outer leaves from the lettuce and wash the rest, leaf by leaf. Shake dry.
2 Peel the onion, place on *a chopping board* and, with *a knife*, slice thinly. Divide into rings.
3 Wash, dry and cut the tomatoes into quarters, removing the hard core.
4 With *a peeler*, peel the cucumber and cut lengthwise into four and then across into cubes with *a knife*.

5 Arrange the salad on to *four plates*.
6 Using your fingers crumble the cheese on top of the salad. With *kitchen scissors*, chop the basil leaves into small pieces and scatter over the cheese. If you like, add the olives.
7 Pour the oil into *a jug*. Add the mustard, lemon juice, salt and pepper. Mix with *a fork* and pour over the Greek salad just before you serve it.

Greek bread with sesame seeds on it is delicious with this salad.

Nutty Tomatoes *(10 years)*

6 large firm tomatoes
150g/6 oz cottage cheese
50g/2 oz raisins
4 pinches salt
4 pinches white pepper
2 teaspoons chopped parsley
75g/3 oz peanuts

1 Wash the tomatoes. With *a knife*, cut off the tops of the tomatoes and set aside.
2 With *a teaspoon*, remove all the tomato pips, being careful not to break the skin. Set the skins to one side and throw away the insides.
3 Place the cottage cheese in *a bowl*. Add the raisins, salt and pepper.
4 Wash the parsley, place in *a mug* and with *kitchen scissors* chop the leaves finely. Add to the cheese mixture.
5 Place the nuts in *a paper bag* and crush them with *a rolling pin*. Add to the mixture in the bowl and stir with *a wooden spoon*.
6 Using a teaspoon, fill the tomato cases with the nutty mixture. Replace the tops of the tomatoes.

Make these nutty tomatoes for lunch or supper or as a 'starter' to a main meal. Just watch how much everyone enjoys them. You'll soon be asked to make them again.

Summer Mousse *(11 years)*

8 tablespoons hot water
2 teaspoons powdered gelatine
½ Knorr chicken stock cube
225g/8 oz curd cheese
½ cucumber
6 radishes
2 spring onions
3 pinches white pepper
1 pinch salt
150ml/¼ pint double cream
a little oil

1 Let *the hot water tap* run for a few seconds until the water is hot and then measure out eight tablespoons into *a jug* or *mug*.* (See below.)
2 Add the gelatine and the ½ chicken stock cube and beat with *a fork* until the gelatine and cube are completely dissolved. Place this jug/mug in *a bowl*, half filled with hot tap water (it mustn't come too near the top of the jug/mug).
3 Place the cheese in *a mixing bowl*.
4 With *a peeler*, peel the cucumber and grate on *a grater* into the cheese.
5 Wash the radishes and trim them with *a knife*. Grate them into the mixing bowl.
6 Wash and trim the spring onions. Place on a *chopping board* and, with the knife, slice finely. Add to the cheese.
7 Add the dissolved gelatine and cube mixture, salt and pepper to the cheese mixture and stir with *a wooden spoon*.
8 In *another bowl*, lightly whip the cream with *a whisk* until it thickens but is still runny.
9 Pour the cream into the mixing bowl with the other ingredients and mix together with the wooden spoon.
10 Grease *a round bowl* with a little oil using a piece of *kitchen paper*.

11 Pour the summer mousse into the oiled bowl and place in the fridge.

12 When set, run *a knife* along the inside edge of the bowl, loosening the mousse. Place *a larger-than-the-bowl plate* over the top of the bowl, facing down. Carefully pick up the bowl and the plate and turn the whole lot upside down, placing the plate on the table and the bowl, now facing down, on top. The mousse should now come away from the bowl (you can give it a gentle tap or two) and sit on the plate.

Either serve this on its own or surround with more radishes and spring onions.

* Check if your hot tap water is safe for drinking. If not, boil an electric kettle, let it cool for 2 minutes and then use the water.

A Country Cottage *(10 years)*

450g/1 lb uncut brown loaf of bread
450g/1 lb cream cheese
mustard and cress
handful of peanuts

Filling One
50g/2 oz softened butter or margarine
50g/2 oz curd or cottage cheese
1 tablespoon chopped chives
1 tablespoon mayonnaise

Filling Two
50g/2 oz softened butter or margarine
50g/2 oz grated cheddar cheese

Filling Three
75g/3 oz cottage cheese
1 tablespoon tomato ketchup
2 tablespoons peanuts

1 Place the bread on *a breadboard*. Cut off all the crusts. Stand bread on its end and slice lengthwise into five slices.
2 On *the kitchen scales*, weigh the butter and cheese for *filling one* and mix in *a bowl* with *a wooden spoon*. Add the chives and mayonnaise.
3 Weigh the butter and cheese for *filling two* and, on *a grater*, grate the cheese. Place in *another bowl* and mix.
4 Weigh the cheese for *filling three*. Place in *a third bowl* and add the tomato ketchup.
5 Place the nuts in *a paper bag* and crush with *a rolling pin*, then add them to the third bowl.
6 Assemble the 'country cottage'. Spread half *filling one* on the bottom slice. Cover with another slice of bread and spread the top of this slice with all of *filling two*.

7 Place the third slice on top, as the next layer, and spread with all of *filling three*.

8 Place the fourth slice on top and spread with the remaining half of *filling one*.

9 Top with the fifth and final slice of bread.

10 Wrap the 'country cottage' in *tin foil* and place in the fridge for one hour.

11 Place the 'cottage' on *a wooden board* and remove the foil. The layers should go sideways across the 'cottage'.

12 Cover the roof and four sides of the 'cottage' with the cream cheese, spread with *a knife*. (If the cheese is too stiff to spread, gradually add milk and mix with a fork until creamy).

13 With *kitchen scissors*, cut the tops of the mustard and cress and sprinkle all over the 'cottage'.

14 With the handful of peanuts, make a door, two windows and a chimney.

To serve, slice as you would a normal loaf of bread.

PUDDINGS

Banana Splits *(9 years)*

125g/4 oz raspberries
4 tablespoons icing sugar
150ml/¼ pint whipping cream
4 bananas
4 scoops vanilla ice cream

1 Make the melba sauce by using *a wooden spoon* to press the raspberries through *a nylon sieve* into *a bowl*.
2 Sift the icing sugar through *a dry sieve* into the bowl with the raspberries. Using *a wooden spoon*, beat the sauce until smooth.
3 Pour the cream into *a bowl* and with *a whisk*, whisk until thick.
4 Peel the bananas. Place each peeled banana on *a plate*. Place a scoop of ice cream next to each banana.
5 Cover the bananas with the melba sauce.
6 Add large dollops of cream on each banana split and eat immediately.

Fresh Fruit Salad *(9 years)*

200g/8 oz black grapes
1 apple
1 pear
2 oranges
2 bananas
100g/4 oz raspberries
2 tablespoons lemon juice
caster sugar

1 Wash the grapes and the apple.
2 With *a knife* cut all the grapes in half and remove all the pips. Place in *a fruit bowl*.
3 Quarter the apple with the knife, remove the core and slice. Add to the grapes.
4 Peel the pear with the knife, quarter it and remove the core and slice. Add to the fruit bowl.
5 Place the oranges on *a chopping board* and with the knife, cut downwards removing the skin and the pith. Slice the flesh thinly, discarding any pips. Add to the fruit bowl.
6 Peel the bananas and slice thickly. Add the banana slices and the raspberries to the other fruit.
7 Pour the lemon juice over the fruit and sprinkle with caster sugar. Mix lightly with *a spoon*.
8 Leave in a fridge for one hour or longer before eating.

You might like some more sugar and some fresh cream with this fruit salad.

Apple Snow (7 years)

1 egg white
130g/4½ oz tin of apple puree

1 Place the egg white in *a bowl* and with *a wire whisk*, whisk until stiff. It is stiff enough when you can turn the bowl upside down without the egg white coming out. Be careful not to spill any if it's *not* stiff enough.
2 Gently add the apple puree, stirring all the time. Stir with the same whisk or *a fork*.
3 Spoon the mixture into *a pretty dish*. There is enough for two small portions or one greedy one.

Sponge fingers go very well with apple snow, or any other little plain biscuits will do.

American Cheesecake (9 years)

225g/8 oz digestive biscuits
100g/4 oz butter
225g/8 oz curd cheese
150ml/5 fl oz double cream
50g/2 oz caster sugar
1 lemon
1 tin of black cherry pie filling (optional)

1 On the *kitchen scales* weigh the biscuits, butter, cheese and sugar.
2 Place the biscuits in *a paper bag* and crush them with *a rolling pin*. Put the crushed biscuits in *a cake tin* with a loose base.
3 With *a knife* cut up the butter and place in a *small bowl*.
4 Half-fill *a larger bowl* with hot tap water and stand the small bowl with butter in it, in the water. Stir the butter until it has melted using *a spoon*.
5 Pour the butter over the crushed biscuits, mix and press down with the back of *a large spoon*. Place in the fridge.
6 Place the cheese, cream and sugar in *a mixing bowl* and mix with *a wooden spoon* until smooth.
7 Wash and dry the lemon and grate the peel very finely on *a grater*. Add the lemon peel to the cheese.
8 Squeeze the lemon on a *lemon squeezer* and add the juice (about two teaspoons) to the cheese.
9 With the wooden spoon cream the cheese mixture until really smooth.
10 Spoon the cheesecake mixture into the cake tin and place in the fridge for one or two hours.
11 Run *a knife* along the inside edge of the tin and carefully remove the cake, pushing up from the bottom. Place on to *a plate*.

You can open a tin of black cherry pie filling and spread it over the top of the cake if you wish.

Raspberry Ice Cream (8 years)

450g/1 lb fresh or thawed frozen raspberries
juice from half a lemon
175g/6 oz icing sugar
300ml/½ pt double cream

1 Rub the raspberries through *a nylon sieve*, using *a wooden spoon*, into *a bowl*.
2 Add the lemon juice and the icing sugar to the raspberry puree.
3 In *another bowl* whip the cream using *a whisk* until quite thick but not too stiff.
4 Gently fold the cream into the puree.
5 Pour this mixture into *a plastic container*. Cover and place in *a freezer*. Leave for four hours.
6 Ten minutes before you want to eat the ice cream, take the container out of the freezer to soften the ice cream a little.

You do not have to use raspberries. Blackberries, loganberries, bilberries, strawberries are all equally delicious. But do not used tinned fruit. It is too sweet.

Apricot Tarts *(8 years)*

425g/15 oz tin of apricot halves
125g/4 oz small digestive biscuits (about 15 biscuits)
100g/3 oz apricot jam
1 teaspoon lemon juice

1 With *a tin opener*, open the tin and drain the apricot halves through *a colander*.
2 Place the biscuits on *a dish*.
3 Place the jam in *a cup* and stir in the lemon juice. Mix well with *a teaspoon*.
4 With *a knife*, spread a little of the jam from the cup on each biscuit.
5 Place the drained apricot halves on top of the biscuits, the rounded side facing up. Spread a little more jam on top of each apricot half.

Have the tarts as a pudding or hand them round at teatime and see them disappear very quickly.

Pretend Eggs *(10 years)*

6 eggs
225g/8 oz curd cheese
1 tablespoon caster sugar
½ teaspoon vanilla essence
tinned apricot-halves

1 Holding one of the eggs firmly but lightly on top of *a plate*, pierce each end of the egg with *a skewer*, making holes but not cracking the egg shell.
2 Blow through one of the holes and let the egg run through the opposite hole into *a bowl*. Repeat with the other eggs. Cover the bowl with cling film and put in the fridge. A grown up may like to use the eggs to make an omelette or scrambled eggs.
3 With *a pair of scissors*, carefully cut off the top off each shell, trying not to crack the rest of the shell.
4 Gently wash the shells in warm water and let them dry.
5 In *a bowl* whip the cheese, sugar and vanilla essence with *a fork* until smooth.
6 Place the shells in *egg cups* and, with *two teaspoons*, fill them with the cheese mixture.
7 With *a tin opener*, open a tin of apricots.
8 Place an apricot-half on top of the cheese mixture in each egg shell.

Chocolate Cake (10 years)

125g/4 oz unsalted butter
250g/8 oz digestive biscuits
75g/3 oz currants
140g/5 oz plain chocolate (Bournville or Menier)
2 tablespoons golden syrup

1 On the *kitchen scales* weigh the butter, biscuits, currants, and chocolate.
2 Grease *a loose-bottomed cake tin* with a little oil, using *a piece of kitchen paper*.
3 Break the chocolate into small pieces and place in *a bowl*.
4 Using *a knife*, cut the butter into small pieces and add to the chocolate.
5 Half-fill *a larger bowl* with hot tap water and place the bowl containing the chocolate and butter in this water.
6 Stir with *a wooden spoon* until both the chocolate and butter have melted. (Note: You may have to change the hot water once or twice before this mixture is totally melted.)
7 Place the biscuits in *a paper bag* and crush them with *a rolling pin*.
8 Add the biscuit crumbs, the syrup and the currants to the melted chocolate and butter mixture.
9 Pour the mixture into the cake tin and, with the back of a wooden spoon, press down evenly and firmly. Leave in the fridge to set.
10 Take the set cake out of the fridge.
11 Run *a knife* round the inside edge of the cake tin to loosen.
12 Place *a large plate*, facing down, over the top of the cake tin. Lift the tin and plate together and turn upside down so the plate is now underneath the tin. Place on the table.
13 Lift the cake tin off the plate, leaving the cake on the plate.
14 Slice into small pieces as this chocolate cake is quite rich.

You can cut this cake into even smaller pieces – the size of chocolates – and serve it to your parents and their friends to have with their coffee after a meal.

Creamy Delight *(10 years)*

1 egg
200g/8 oz curd cheese
8 teaspoons double cream
1 lemon
25g/1 oz mixed peel
1 tablespoon caster sugar
6 drops vanilla essence

1 Crack the egg against *a cup* to break the shell. Separate the egg white from the yolk, letting the egg white drop in *a bowl* and putting the yolk in the cup.
2 Place the cheese, the egg yolk and the cream in *a mixing bowl* and beat with *a wooden spoon* until the mixture is smooth.
3 Wash and dry the lemon. Grate the rind on *a fine grater* into the cheese and cream mixture.
4 Place the lemon on *a chopping board* and, with *a knife*, cut in half.
5 Squeeze on *a lemon squeezer* and add 1 *teaspoon* of the juice to the cheese and cream mixture.
6 Add the mixed peel, sugar and vanilla essence and mix with the wooden spoon.
7 With *a whisk*, whisk the egg white and, when stiff, add it to the creamy mixture. Mix well with the wooden spoon.
8 Spoon the creamy delight into *little pots*.

Have some sponge fingers or 'cats' tongues' with this pudding. This is a simple version of a Russian pudding eaten at Christmas-time. It is called Pashka.

Nursery Pudding (any age)

1 125ml/5 oz tub double cream
1 250ml/10 oz tub natural yogurt
soft dark brown sugar
8 walnut halves

1 Pour the cream into *a bowl*.
2 With *a fork* whisk the yogurt in with the cream.
3 Pour the mixture into *a dish*.
4 Cover thickly with the brown sugar.
5 Place the walnuts on top.
6 Put in the fridge for 1 hour and serve cold.

Yogurt Fruit Mousse (8 years)

300g/8 oz fresh fruit such as strawberries, raspberries or
  blackberries
150ml/¼ pint thick-set natural yogurt or double cream
3 tablespoons caster sugar
whites from 2 eggs

1 Pick over the fruit and throw away any bad berries.
2 Take the green tops off the strawberries, if you are using
  them.
3 Place the fruit in *a bowl*, add the sugar and mash with *a fork*.
4 Using *a wooden spoon* press the fruit through *a nylon sieve* into
  another bowl to get rid of all the pips.
5 Add the yogurt or cream and mix with the wooden spoon.
6 In *another bowl*, whisk the egg whites using *a whisk* until they
  are very stiff.
7 Fold the egg whites into the fruit and yogurt mixture.
8 Spoon into *a dish* and place in the fridge for 2 hours.

Make this pudding when there are some spare egg whites. To
check the correct amount of egg whites weigh them on the
kitchen scales. Each egg white weighs about 25g/1 oz.

Banana Hedgehogs *(6 years)*

8 teaspoons apricot jam
1 teaspoon water
4 medium-sized bananas
8 tablespoons dessicated coconut
1 handful split almonds
12 currants

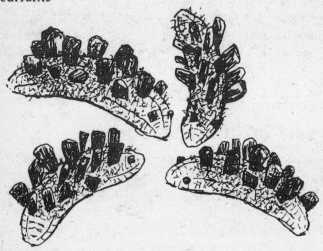

1 Mix jam and water in *a bowl*.
2 Rub this mixture through *a sieve* on to *a plate* using *a wooden spoon*.
3 Peel the bananas and, using *a small knife*, spread the jam over them.
4 Place the coconut on *another plate* and roll the jam-covered bananas in the coconut.
5 Arrange bananas on *a dish* and cover with the split almonds in a hedgehog fashion.
6 Place the currants so they look like the eyes and nose of each hedgehog.

Honey Cream (7 years)

150ml/¼ pint double cream
2 teaspoons lemon juice
2 dessertspoons runny honey

1 Pour the cream into *a bowl* and whisk with *a whisk* until thick but still runny. Whisk in the lemon juice.
2 Add the honey, stirring lightly with *a fork*.
3 Spoon it into *2 sweet dishes*, or serve it with strawberries or raspberries.

Redcurrants with Banana Sauce (8 years)

250g/8 oz redcurrants
2 ripe bananas
3 tablespoons caster sugar
125ml/¼ pint single cream
1 tablespoon lemon juice

1 Wash the redcurrants.
2 Hold the stalk firmly in one hand and slide *a fork* along the stalk, gently removing all the redcurrants into *a dish*. (This is easier than using your fingers to remove the currants one by one.)
3 Lightly mash the currants with the fork.
4 Peel the bananas and place in *a bowl*. Mash until smooth.
5 Add the sugar, cream and lemon juice to the bananas and mix with *a spoon*. Spoon this banana mixture over the redcurrants.

It is best to eat this pudding immediately. The bananas turn brown if left too long.

Chocolate Log Cake (10 years)

1 orange
300ml/½ pint double cream
2 dessertspoons drinking chocolate powder
8 drops vanilla essence
1 packet chocolate chip biscuits

1 With *a lemon squeezer* squeeze the orange and pour the juice into *a dish*.
2 Whip the cream lightly in *a bowl* using *a whisk*. The cream should be soft and thick, but not runny.
3 Add the vanilla essence and the chocolate powder to the cream and mix it in with *a wooden spoon*.
4 Find *a dish* or tray for your cake.
5 Dip each biscuit into the orange juice. Stick them together with dollops of cream mixture, piling one on top of the other. When all the biscuits are used up lay them sideways on the dish or tray to look like a log.
6 Cover with the rest of the cream mixture.
7 Draw *a fork* over the top and along the sides to form a wavy pattern.

You don't have to wait until Christmas to make this delicious cake. For a different log cake, use different types of biscuits such as gingernuts, leaving the drinking chocolate out of the recipe.

Lemon and Ginger Crunch *(10 years)*

200g/8 oz ginger biscuits
100g/4 oz unsalted butter
1 lemon
400g/14 fl oz tin of sweetened condensed milk
2 tablespoons double cream

1 Weight the biscuits and the butter on *the kitchen scales*.
2 With *a knife* cut the butter into little pieces and place in *a small bowl*.
3 Half-fill *a larger bowl* with *hot tap water* and place the bowl with the butter in it into the water.
4 Stir the butter until it has melted using *a spoon*.
5 Place the biscuits in *a paper bag* and crush them with *a rolling pin*.
6 Place the crushed biscuits in *a cake tin* and pour the butter over them. Mix and press firmly down using the back of *a wooden spoon*. Place the tin in the fridge.
7 Wash the lemon, dry it and, on *a fine grater*, grate the skin into *a mixing bowl*.
8 Cut the lemon in half with *a knife* and, with *a squeezer*, squeeze the juice. Add this juice to the mixing bowl.
9 With *a tin opener*, open the tin of condensed milk and pour into the bowl.
10 With *a whisk*, whisk the mixture until thick (about 5 minutes). Add the cream and whisk a little longer.
11 Pour the mixture on to the crushed biscuit base and return to the fridge.

This is a soft cake and, with keeping, it gets very gooey.

Orange Clowns *(10 years)*

oranges (one per person)
smarties
ice cream
ice cream cones (one per person)

1 On *a chopping board* slice the top off each orange, using *a knife*.
2 With *a teaspoon* remove the pulp into *a bowl*.
3 With *kitchen scissors* cut a slit in the empty orange case for the mouth and pierce three holes for the eyes and nose.
4 Place smarties in place of eyes and nose.
5 With *a fork* remove all the pith and pips from the orange flesh. Mix the left-over juice with the ice cream and put into the orange cases. Place in a freezer.
6 Take the orange clowns out of the freezer ten minutes before eating.
7 When ready to eat, place a cone on each orange for a hat.

You can prepare the orange clowns well in advance of eating them.

Strawberry Ice Cream Cake *(10 years)*

8 trifle sponge cakes
1 orange
1 family size brick of ice cream
225g/8 oz strawberries (fresh or frozen)
300ml/½ pint whipping cream

1 With *a knife*, carefully split the cakes in half.
2 Line base and sides of *a one kilogram/2½ lb loaf tin* with the cakes, the cut sides towards the centre. (Some of the halves will have to be cut to fit the empty edges of the tin.) Keep four halves for the top.
3 Cut the orange in half with *a knife* and, with *a lemon squeezer*, squeeze the orange halves.
4 Pour the juice over the cakes.
5 Fill the centre with ice cream.
6 Place the four reserved sponge cakes on top.
7 Cover with *tin foil* and leave in the freezer for three hours.
8 Take the tops off the strawberries and slice them, using a knife.
9 Pour the cream into *a bowl* and whisk it until thick, using *a wire whisk*.
10 Take the cake out of the freezer, turn out on to *a plate*, cover with the whipped cream and the strawberries.

Peach Melba (8 years)

1 425g/15 oz tin of peach halves
150ml/5 fl oz double cream
275g/10 oz block vanilla ice cream
3 tablespoons seedless raspberry jam
wafer biscuits

1 With *a tin opener*, open the tin of peaches and, with *a draining spoon*, lift them on to *a plate*.
2 Pour the cream into *a bowl* and whisk with *a whisk* until thick but not runny.
3 Divide the ice cream between *four glass dishes*.
4 Place two peach-halves in each dish. Spoon some jam over them and add a spoonful of cream on top.
5 Place one wafer biscuit in each dish.

If the jam is very thick dilute with a tablespoon of peach juice.

Banana Surprise (any age)

4 bananas
300ml/½ pint single cream
drinking chocolate

1 Place the bananas on *a dish* and, using *a fork*, mash them very well.
2 Add the cream and gently beat the two together with the fork.
3 Cover with drinking chocolate powder so that no banana mixture is showing.

Orange Surprise *(any age)*

1 small tin of frozen, concentrated orange juice
3 small pots of plain yogurt

1 Let the orange juice thaw.
2 Pour the yogurt into a bowl and mix in the orange juice, using *a fork*.
3 Pour into *glasses* and eat with sponge fingers.

SWEETS FOR PRESENTS

Brandy Truffles *(10 years)*

2 tablespoons brandy
125g/4 oz plain chocolate
40g/1½ oz unsalted butter
50g/2 oz icing sugar
50g/2 oz ground almonds
50g/2 oz grated plain chocolate

1 Carefully weigh all the ingredients (except for the brandy) on *the kitchen scales.*
2 Break the chocolate into pieces and place in *a large bowl.*
3 Half-fill *a pan* with *hot tap water* and place the bowl with chocolate in the pan. Stir with *a wooden spoon* until melted. (You may have to change the hot tap water once or twice.)
4 Add the other ingredients except the grated chocolate and mix well. Leave in a cold place until firm.
5 Place the grated chocolate on *a large plate.*
6 With your hands (make sure they are very clean) form the cooled mixture into little balls and roll in the grated chocolate.
7 Place each ball in *a sweet-paper case.* There will be about 16 balls (truffles). Keep in a cool place until ready to eat.

You can place the truffles in a pretty box and give them as a very special Christmas present.

Chocolate Krispies (7 years)

75g/3 oz Rice Krispies
125g/4 oz milk chocolate
2 tablespoons seedless raisins

1 On *the kitchen scales*, weigh the chocolate and the Rice Krispies.
2 Break the chocolate into pieces and place in *a small bowl*.
3 Half-fill *a larger bowl* with *hot tap water* and stand the bowl with the chocolate in it in the water.
4 Stir with *a spoon* until the chocolate has melted.
5 Place the Rice Krispies and raisins in *a mixing bowl*. Add the melted chocolate, stirring with a spoon until both the Rice Krispies and the raisins are well coated.
6 Lightly oil *a cake tin or a flan dish* with a little oil using *a piece of kitchen paper towel*.
7 Spoon the mixture into the dish and, with your hands, push down well, flattening the top.
8 Cool in the fridge and then, with *a knife*, cut into squares or long strips.

Lemon Coconut Kisses *(8 years)*

1 tablespoon evaporated milk
1 tablespoon lemon juice (or juice from half a lemon)
100g/4 oz icing sugar
75g/3 oz dessicated coconut
4 drops red food colouring

1 Pour the evaporated milk and lemon juice into *a mixing bowl*.
2 On *the kitchen scales* weigh the sugar and the coconut. Add both to the mixing bowl.
3 Add 4 drops of food colouring and, using *a wooden spoon*, mix everything well until the mixture looks like a soft ball.
4 With your hands break off little pieces of the ball. Roll each piece so it looks like a small sausage. Press two sausages together to form a kiss, the sort of kiss you would sign at the bottom of a letter (×).
5 Place the kisses on *a tray* and leave to harden a little in a cool place or in the fridge.

These delicious pink 'kisses' can be given as presents. Just place each one in a sweet-paper case and place the cases in a box. You will have about 36 kisses.

Coconut Ice *(8 years)*

2 egg whites
450g/1 lb icing sugar
2 tablespoons water
175g/6 oz dessicated coconut
red food colouring

1 Place the egg whites in *a bowl*, and whisk using *a wire whisk* until frothy.
2 Weigh the sugar on *the kitchen scales* and add to the egg whites. Stir with *a wooden spoon*. Slowly add the water.
3 Weigh the coconut and add it to the sugar and egg white mixture. Mix well.
4 Using *a piece of kitchen paper*, lightly grease *a cake tin* with a little oil.
5 Spread half the coconut mixture in the cake tin.
6 Add *a teaspoon* of red food colouring to the rest of coconut mixture left in the bowl. Mix well.
7 Spread the pink coconut ice on top of the white.
8 Leave the coconut ice in the fridge to set. Cut into squares.

Place the coconut ice in a box or a pretty bag. Everyone will appreciate such a delicious present.

Coloured Sugar Eggs *(9 years)*

4 tablespoons evaporated milk
450g/1 lb icing sugar
green, red and blue food colouring

1 With *a tin opener* open the tin of evaporated milk and pour
   out 4 *tablespoons* into *a mixing bowl*.
2 Weigh the sugar on *the kitchen scales*. Sift the sugar through
   a sieve, gradually adding it to the milk.
3 Beat the sugar and the milk with *a wooden spoon*. If it is
   difficult, finish mixing with your hands.
4 Pick up one third of the mixture and place on a clean
   surface. Add ten drops of red colouring and knead it with
   your hands until smooth.
5 Take half of the remaining mixture from the bowl and add
   ten green drops of colouring. Knead well until smooth.
6 Add the ten blue drops of colouring to the mixture left in
   the bowl and knead well.
7 Break off little pieces and shape into coloured eggs.

These little eggs are perfect to put in a pretty dish on the
dining table at Easter time. Or pack them in a transparent box
or bag and give as presents.

Peppermint Cream Mice *(8 years)*

170g/6 oz condensed milk
170g/6 oz softened butter
¼ teaspoon peppermint essence
400g/14 oz icing sugar
currants
flaked almonds
angelica

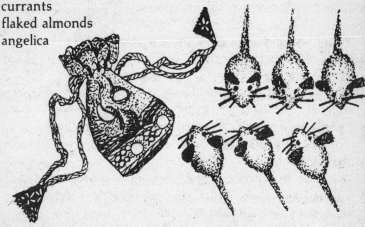

1 Weigh the butter and sugar on *the kitchen scales*.
2 Put the condensed milk, butter and peppermint essence in *a mixing bowl* and mix with *a wooden spoon*. Gradually add the sugar, mixing all the time.
3 Sprinkle more icing sugar on a working surface. Place the mixture on top of the working surface and, using your hands, knead until smooth.
4 Pick off little pieces of the kneaded mixture and, in your hands, form little rounded mice. Make a thin tail at one end and a pointed face at the other.
5 Put all the mice (about 24) on *a tray*.
6 Use currants for the eyes and flaked almonds for the ears.
7 With *a knife* cut thin slithers from a piece of angelica and use these for the whiskers.
8 Cover the tray with *a clean tea towel* and leave the mice in a cool place to dry.

Place the mice in pretty bags tied with ribbons at the top and give as presents.

Chocolate Coconut Squares *(9 years)*

5 tablespoons sweetened condensed milk
125g/4 oz dessicated coconut
125g/4 oz caster sugar
pinch of tartar
1 125g/4 oz bar milk or plain chocolate

1 Pour the condensed milk into *a mixing bowl.*
2 On *the kitchen scales* weigh the sugar and the coconut and add with a pinch of tartar to the condensed milk.
3 Mix well with *a wooden spoon* until the mixture sticks together.
4 With a little oil and using *some kitchen paper,* oil *a square, oval or rectangular dish or tin* and press the mixture into it. Place in the fridge.
5 Break up the chocolate and place in *a small bowl.*
6 Fill *a larger bowl* with *hot tap water* and place the bowl with the chocolate in it in the hot water. Stir with *a fork* until melted.
7 Using *a knife,* spread the melted chocolate over the coconut in the tin. Leave in the fridge until firm. Cut into squares.

Milky Way Fudge *(9 years)*

175g/6 oz white chocolate
180ml/5 fl oz sweetened condensed milk
15ml/½ fl oz water
1 teaspoon vanilla essence

1 On *the kitchen scales* weigh the white chocolate. Break the chocolate into little pieces and place in *a bowl*.
2 Pour some *hot tap water* into *a larger bowl* and stand the bowl with the chocolate in it in the hot water. Stir with *a wooden spoon* until melted. (You may have to change the hot water once or twice.)
3 Remove the bowl from the hot water and add the condensed milk to the melted chocolate.
4 Add the water and the vanilla essence to the bowl.
5 With *kitchen paper*, grease *a baking tin* with some oil.
6 Spread the fudge mixture in the tin. Leave in the fridge or a cold place to set.
7 When set, cut into small squares.

Put the fudge squares into pretty boxes or bags. Tie with a coloured ribbon and give somebody a delicious present.

DRINKS

Thick Chocolate Shake *(any age)*

300ml/½ pint milk
6 rounded tablespoons chocolate ice cream
1 tablespoon chocolate syrup or chocolate dessert sauce
grated chocolate

1 Place all the ingredients except the grated chocolate in *a tall jug* and, using *a whisk*, whisk until smooth and frothy.
2 Pour into *two glasses* and sprinkle some grated chocolate on top.

Minty Chocolate Drink *(any age)*

300ml/½ pint milk
4 tablespoons vanilla ice cream
1 tablespoon milk chocolate powder
½ teaspoon peppermint essence

1 Place everything in *a tall jug* and, with *a whisk*, whisk until smooth and frothy.
2 Place in *two tall glasses*. Drink through *a straw*.

Creamy Milk Shake *(any age)*

300ml/½ pint milk
4 tablespoons vanilla ice cream
whipped cream

1 Place the milk and ice cream in *a tall jug* and whisk with *a whisk* until smooth and frothy.
2 Pour into *two tall glasses* and put a dollop of cream on top of each shake.

Strawberry Shake *(any age)*

300ml/½ pint milk
150ml/¼ pint strawberry yogurt
2 tablespoons strawberry ice cream
2 strawberries (optional)

1 Place everything except the two strawberries in *a tall jug* and whisk, with *a whisk*, until smooth and frothy.
2 Pour into *two tall glasses*, place a strawberry on top of each and drink through *a thick straw*.

Ice Cream Soda *(any age)*

vanilla ice cream
fizzy lemonade or cola

1 Place one heaped tablespoon vanilla ice cream in *a tall glass*.
2 Fill with fizzy lemonade or cola and drink through *a straw*.

Banana Milk Shake *(any age)*

1 ripe banana
300ml/½ pint milk
4 tablespoons vanilla ice cream

1 Peel the banana and mash on *a plate* with *a fork*.
2 Place the mashed banana in *a tall jug*.
3 Add the ice cream and pour in the milk.
4 Whisk with *a whisk* until thick and frothy and pour into *two tall glasses*.

Blackberry Milk Shake *(7 years)*

1 cupful freshly picked blackberries
300ml/½ pint milk
1 small pot of natural yogurt
2 tablespoons vanilla ice cream

1 Wash the blackberries.
2 Rub the blackberries through *a nylon sieve* into *a tall jug* using *a wooden spoon*.
3 Add the milk, yogurt and ice cream to the blackberry puree and whisk with *a whisk* until frothy.
4 Pour into *two tall glasses*.

Orange Yogurt Shake (8 years)

2 oranges
300ml/½ pint natural yogurt
2 tablespoon runny honey

1 With *a knife* cut the oranges in half.
2 Squeeze the oranges on *a squeezer* and pour the juice into *a tall jug*.
3 Add the yogurt and the honey and stir with *a long spoon* until smooth.
4 Pour into two glasses and drink immediately.

You should drink this shake at once because oranges lose their vitamin C goodness very rapidly after being squeezed.

Egg Nog (7 years)

300ml/½ pint milk
1 teaspoon caster sugar
1 egg
powdered nutmeg

1 Pour the milk into *a tall jug*. Add the sugar.
2 Break the egg against *a cup* and add the raw egg to the milk.
3 Using *a whisk*, whisk until frothy.
4 Pour into *two glasses* and sprinkle some nutmeg on top.

For the grown-ups you can add a tablespoon of brandy or rum to the milk. It will warm them up on a cold, frosty day.

Orange Strawberry Shake *(7 years)*

125g/4 oz strawberries
300ml/½ pint yogurt
1 small glass pure orange juice
1 tablespoon runny honey
2 tablespoons vanilla ice cream

1 Take off the green tops of the strawberries and place the strawberries on *a plate*.
2 Mash them with *a fork* and place the strawberry puree in *a tall jug*.
3 Add the yogurt, orange juice, honey and vanilla ice cream.
4 Whisk with *a whisk* until smooth and frothy and pour into *two or three glasses*.
5 Drink through *a thick straw*.

Blackcurrant Milk Shake *(any age)*

300ml/½ pint milk
6 tablespoons vanilla ice cream
2–4 tablespoons blackcurrant juice

1 Pour the milk and the ice cream into *a jug* and, using *a whisk*, whisk until thick and frothy. Add the blackcurrant juice.
2 Stir and pour into *two glasses*. (Some blackcurrant juices are stronger than others, so you won't need so much of them.)